BE A WARRIOR

NOT A WORRIER

How to De-Stress and Cope with Anxiety Naturally

ELIZABETH ARCHER

First Published by Summersdale Publishers Ltd, an imprint of Hachette UK, 2018.

First Racehorse Publishing edition, 2019.

Elizabeth Archer has asserted her moral right to be identified as the author of this work in accordance with sections 77 and 78 of the Copyright, Designs and Patents Act 1988.

Racehorse Publishing books may be purchased in bulk at special discounts for sales promotion, corporate gifts, fund-raising, or educational purposes. Special editions can also be created to specifications. For details, contact the Special Sales Department, Skyhorse Publishing, 307 West 36th Street, 11th Floor, New York, NY 10018 or info@skyhorsepublishing.com.

Racehorse Publishing™ is a pending trademark of Skyhorse Publishing, Inc.®, a Delaware corporation.

Visit our website at www.skyhorsepublishing.com.

10 9 8 7 6 5 4 3 2 1

Library of Congress Cataloging-in-Publication Data is available on file.

Design by Luci Ward

ISBN: 978-1-63158-433-6
E-Book ISBN: 978-1-63158-442-8

Printed in China

CONTENTS

Introduction...4

Coping With Anxiety................................6

How to De-Stress Your Work Day........................27

How to De-Stress Your Home............................48

Eat Well, Feel Well 68

Get Fit, Get Happy....................................87

Sleep Well, Feel Well................................104

Be Positive..124

Slow Down..144

Natural Therapies....................................161

Seeking Help...180

Introduction

Think back to the last time you felt truly calm and in control. Perhaps it was a day last week when you finished all your work on time, or when you were trusted with an important task that you knew you could do well. Perhaps you remembered to do something you often forget, like making your bed. Whenever it was, it's probably a feeling you'd like to have more frequently. All too often, our busy lives mean that this feeling of inner calm is spoiled, whether we're worrying about our jobs, money, our family and friends, or the thought of getting out of bed in the morning. While we can't always change the things that make us feel stressed, we don't have to let those things worry us so much. This book will give you simple, practical ways to arm yourself for the battlefield of everyday life so you can take on each new challenge with the strength and assurance of a warrior.

THE POWER OF THE MIND

We often underestimate it, but our mind is the most powerful weapon we have when it comes to battling fear and anxiety. However, in order for it to work as it should, we have to look after it like any other part of the body: with the right foods, plenty of sleep, and enough exercise to keep it strong and agile.

COPING

WITH

ANXIETY

BREATHE

If you feel anxiety mounting and your heart pumping, take a moment to yourself. Close your eyes and breathe deeply through your nose for five counts, then breathe out through your mouth for seven counts. Do this ten times. This will help to center you and prevent your feelings from spiraling.

TOO MANY OF US ARE
NOT LIVING OUR

dreams

BECAUSE WE ARE LIVING OUR

fears.

LES BROWN

GO FOR A WALK

If things are getting on top of
you, take 5 minutes out to go for
a walk. Whatever the weather,
and wherever you are, getting
outside and breathing fresh air is
a proven way to relieve feelings
of stress and tension. Plus, it will
help to improve your mood as
the gentle exercise will release
serotonin, the happy hormone.

PHONE A FRIEND

Sometimes hearing a familiar voice is all you need to put your mind at rest. If you're feeling tense, make a quick call to a friend or family member. You could talk about how you feel, as sharing with a loved one can often ease any burden you are feeling. Or you could chat about something completely different to take a break from your worries and focus your mind elsewhere.

THERE ARE
MANY WAYS
OF GETTING
STRONG.
SOMETIMES
TALKING IS
THE BEST WAY.

Andre Agassi

MAKE A PLAN

When we're anxious, it's sometimes
hard to think about anything other
than getting through the day. Take
your mind off your worries by planning
something, such as going to the movies
with a friend, going out for breakfast,
or thinking about something in your day
or week that you're looking forward to,
even if it's as small as having a cup of tea
when you get home. This will give you
something else to focus on when you're
feeling stressed and redirect your mind
to something more positive.

When everything seems to be going against you, remember that the airplane takes off against the wind, not with it.

Henry Ford

Writing down your feelings can be a powerful way of putting them to rest. If your mind is still whirring before bed, try jotting down whatever happened in your day and how you feel about it, or any worries that you have. Sometimes just the simple act of writing can be cathartic and calming.

KEEP A JOURNAL

DO
your thing
AND DON'T CARE
IF THEY
like it.

Tina Fey

FACE YOUR FEARS

We all know the feeling: you've made a mistake at work and are dreading telling your boss, or you have to make that call to a friend to let them down, so you put it off as long as possible. But this delaying tactic can make your anxiety worse, as you end up spending your time worrying about the outcome and imagining the worst-case scenario. Whatever it is you're avoiding, face your fear and tackle the problem head-on. Once you've done it you'll feel relieved that you are in control of the situation and the worries about all the possible outcomes will disappear.

ROLL YOUR SHOULDERS

When you're anxious, the muscles in your body
tense up and your shoulders tend to rise. Next
time you are feeling stressed, try rolling your
shoulders down. This posture will open your chest
and help you breathe more easily, which will help
to put you back into a relaxed frame of mind.

Your mind is your prison when you focus on your fear.

Tim Fargo

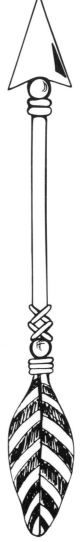

SWITCH

It's great to feel connected to the people you love, but sometimes our phones can be a source of stress instead of support. If the notifications from that group message are driving you crazy, or you feel worried because you haven't replied to your friend immediately, just give yourself a break. Turn off your phone for a few hours and put it somewhere out of sight so you're not tempted to switch it back on again. Or, even better, schedule a regular "phone vacation" into your day—perhaps in the afternoon when you're rushing to finish whatever you're doing, or for a few hours in the evening to give you a window of quiet time.

Help
someone else

Giving up your time for someone else may not seem like the obvious thing to do when you're stressed, but lending a helping hand can really give you a boost. This is because

it helps you keep your problems in perspective

and

can also give you a sense of fulfillment

which you don't get from focusing on yourself. Search online for charity projects you could get involved in, or start raising money for a worthy cause. You could also look closer to home—have a cup of tea with a lonely neighbor, for instance, or offer to do the shopping for someone who finds it hard to leave the house. Whatever you do, you'll feel better for it.

Take the day

one step

at a time.

HOW TO DE-STRESS YOUR WORK DAY

Realize you're good enough

We all feel like we're winging it sometimes, whether we're studying, working, applying for jobs, or being a parent. But constantly telling yourself that you're not good enough can become a self-fulfilling prophecy. Next time you find yourself questioning whether you're really qualified for your job, or if you know enough to pass an exam, take a moment to list three recent achievements you're proud of. Don't indulge any negative thoughts which might be pecking at your confidence. If you're still not convinced, it might help to ask someone you admire whether they ever feel as though they're making it up as they go along—the chances are they'll say *yes!*

WHAT YOU DO TODAY CAN IMPROVE ALL YOUR TOMORROWS.

Ralph Marston

TAKE A LUNCH BREAK

However busy your day, make sure you take a lunch break to refresh your mind. You could go for a walk, sit down to eat with a friend, listen to a podcast, or browse the shops. This will help to clear your mind, making you feel calmer and more in control for the rest of the day.

LISTEN
more

Disagreements are one of our biggest sources of stress, but they don't have to be. Next time you disagree with someone, stop and really listen. Try to see their opinion as equal but different instead of "wrong." Doing this will help you to take a step back and approach conversation with the other person in a much calmer frame of mind.

PROCRASTINATION

IS THE

THIEF

OF

TIME

—COLLAR HIM.

Charles Dickens

FIND A MENTOR, BE A MENTOR

What do you dream of achieving in your working, professional, or academic life? Whatever it is, building a support network can help you realize it. Find someone you admire—a teacher, friend, or acquaintance —and ask them if they'll consider giving you some advice and inspiration. They don't need to give up much time —perhaps just a coffee meeting or a video chat every few months. Look outside your place of study or work. It might help to join a networking or support group nearby. If you already have experience, think about becoming a mentor to someone else too—perhaps a younger person or someone who's just starting out in their career. Realizing the value of your knowledge and experience can give you a real confidence boost.

Take an email break

Constantly replying to emails can make you feel anxious when you have other things to do. Instead, you could set aside half an hour or so twice a day to reply and then close the window on your computer. Or if it's not possible to take a complete break, try turning off your on-screen notifications so that you can concentrate fully on tasks without being disturbed by incoming messages.

Don't count the days, make the days count.

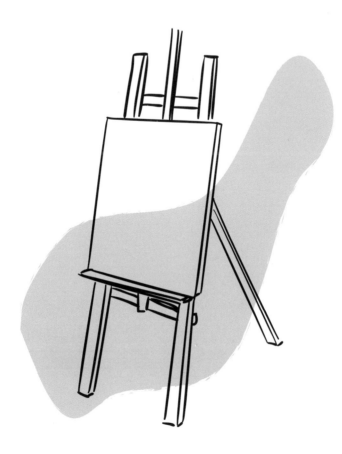

The only way to do great work
is to love what you do.

Steve Jobs

DO THE WORST THINGS FIRST

If you have a towering to-do list and no idea where to start, try doing the most-dreaded jobs first. Not only will ticking them off give you a sense of achievement and spur you on to tackle easier things, but the rest of the day will be free of the worry that comes from looming tasks.

It's hard to beat
a person who

never
gives up.

Babe Ruth

Be 10 minutes early

Rushing from one thing to the next can leave you feeling anxious and exhausted. Next time you have to be somewhere at a given time, aim to get there 10 minutes early. You'll arrive feeling calmer and more in control.

FAR AND AWAY

THE BEST PRIZE

THAT LIFE OFFERS IS THE
CHANCE TO WORK HARD
AT WORK WORTH DOING.

Theodore Roosevelt

Tune in

A great playlist can help you chill out when things get frantic or give you an energy boost to get you through the post-lunch dip. Try classical music if you have a creative task to do, or something more up-tempo if you're tired.

KEEP IT IN PERSPECTIVE

We all have days when we're feeling worried or tired, but most of the time they're mixed in with good days too. Next time you're feeling low, try to keep a sense of perspective by reminding yourself that today is just one day in many. If you're having a bad month or even a bad year, it's time to take a moment and think about what the problem could be.

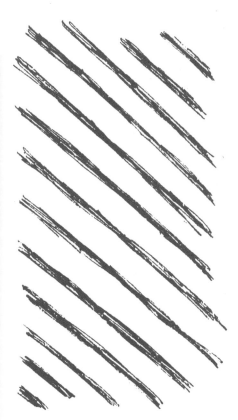

Perhaps a friend or colleague is getting you down, or you're not as passionate about your studies or your job as you used to be.

Whatever the issue, identifying it is the first step; after that, you can make a plan to tackle it.

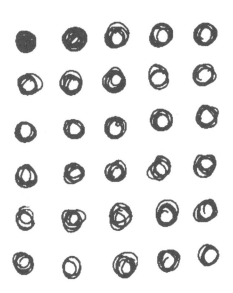

HOW TO DE-STRESS YOUR HOME

Declutter

When you're in a messy space, your stress
levels instantly rise. Try to make your home a
sanctuary. A good way to start is by throwing
away anything you haven't used in the last six
months, and invest in some storage to keep
the rest of your things organized. You don't
have to do the whole house at once—pick
one room to declutter, or even a corner of
a room to start with. Even 5 to 10 minutes
of tidying will help to bring you calm.

Unclutter
your life.
Unclutter
your home.

We feel best when everything and everyone around us is in harmony and in balance.

Eileen Anglin

Home is
NOT A PLACE
but a feeling.

SORT YOUR *Finances*

Often one of our biggest sources of worry is money, but it doesn't have to be. Making a budget for the month and sticking to it can go a long way towards reducing stress. Your first priority should be calculating the money you need to live on, which must cover things such as rent and food. Use what's left to pay off any debt, or if you don't have debt, start a savings account and put aside as much as you can afford. *Ideally* you should have enough money saved to survive on for two or three months in case anything happens to your job or home, but every bit helps.

Create an indoor jungle

One of the easiest and cheapest ways to de-stress your home is to invest in some potted plants. Not only do they look great and brighten a room, but they also absorb pollutants from the air, meaning you can breathe more easily and feel better.

Have nothing in your house that you do not know to be useful or believe to be beautiful.

William Morris

DO A DEEP CLEAN

When was the last time
you gave your home a
really good scrub? Set aside
some time to clean your
house from top to bottom.
Cleansing your living space
will bring you a sense of
calm and having a hygienic
home can help to prevent
allergies from flaring up,
so you'll feel better both
in body and mind.

Make your HOME a place of PEACE.

Light a candle

Have you ever caught a whiff of a particular scent, like your mom's perfume perhaps, and been instantly transported to a vivid memory? That's because smells are strongly associated with emotion in our brains through the limbic system. You can use this to your advantage by filling your home with comforting aromas which instantly make you feel more relaxed. Look for scented candles or diffusers with lavender or jasmine, as these fragrances are both calming. If you want an energizing boost in the morning, try one with citrus notes. Experiment with different scents and rotate them so you don't become desensitized to them.

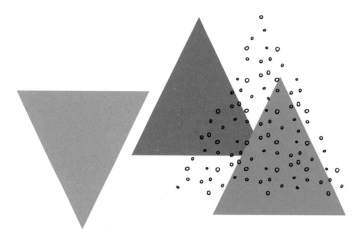

HE IS THE HAPPIEST, BE HE KING OR PEASANT, WHO FINDS PEACE IN HIS HOME.

Johann Wolfgang von Goethe

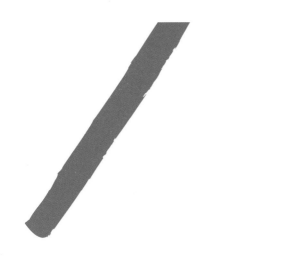

PUT UP PHOTOS

Photographs are a great way
to remind yourself of treasured
memories and make yourself feel
good. Why not get a length of
twine and peg Polaroids or prints
along it? You could then drape it
over a mirror or wrap it around
your bedposts if sticking things on
walls is a no-no.

GET IN
THE ZONE

Open-plan living might be the norm, but dividing your home into different zones for cooking, relaxing, working, and sleeping can help you to unwind. This is because your mind creates a strong association between certain spaces and how you feel in them. For instance, as soon as you step into your bedroom, ideally you'll feel more chilled out and ready for sleep. If you have to mix work and play, like having a desk in your bedroom, try to create a divide between the two areas of the room using a curtain or screen. If you're able to paint your room you could even have a different color scheme in different areas of the room to distinguish them.

HOME IS
WHERE
THE
HEART
IS.

STREAMLINE YOUR WARDROBE

Do you ever look in your wardrobe and think you have tons of clothes but nothing to wear? If so, it might be time for a clear out. That way, you can de-stress your mornings by reaching into your wardrobe and pulling out whatever comes to hand. Start taking everything out of your closet and donating or trashing anything you haven't worn in the last year. Then, pick out the items you love most and hang them up. You could even introduce a color scheme so all your clothes go together.

A MAN TRAVELS
THE WORLD OVER
IN SEARCH OF
WHAT HE NEEDS
AND RETURNS
HOME TO FIND IT.

George Moore

EAT WELL, FEEL WELL

One cannot

think well,

love well,

sleep well,

if one has not

 well.

Virginia Woolf

The most important meal

It can be hard to find the time for breakfast between rolling out of bed and sprinting for the bus. But a healthy morning meal is one of the best ways to keep your mind and body on top form, as it regulates your blood sugar, which steadies your mood and dampens mid-morning cravings for sugary snacks. Try a bowl of oatmeal, fruit and yogurt, or scrambled eggs with toast for a healthy start to the day.

The Magic Mineral

Did you know you can eat your way to a calmer mind? Spinach, pumpkin seeds, chickpeas, avocado, and wholegrains like brown rice and quinoa are all great for busting stress thanks to their naturally high levels of magnesium. When the brain gets a boost from this essential mineral, the levels of stress hormones, such as adrenaline and cortisol, drop, making you feel less anxious. For a stress-busting salad that takes minutes to make, toss grilled chicken or tofu and quinoa with dark leafy greens, avocado, and a drop of olive oil. You could even sprinkle on some pumpkin seeds for extra mood-boosting magnesium.

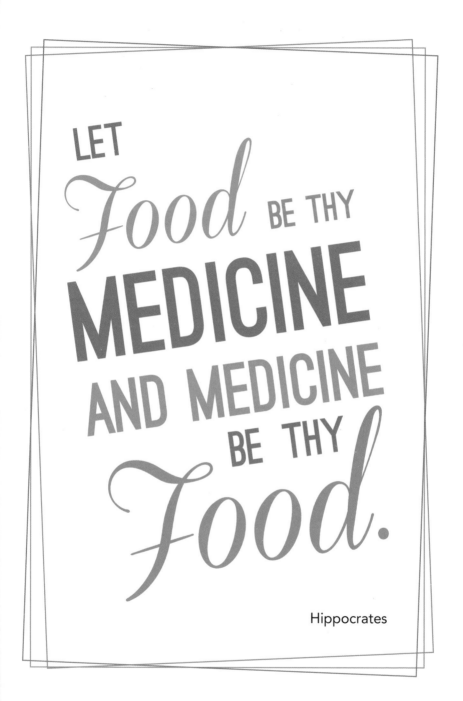

LET *Food* BE THY MEDICINE AND MEDICINE BE THY *Food.*

Hippocrates

WIND DOWN—
DON'T WINE DOWN

After a long day it's tempting to sink into the sofa with a giant glass of wine. But alcohol changes the levels of the happy hormone, serotonin, in the brain and can lead to increased anxiety. Next time you feel like having a drink, think about the situation. Who are you with? How are you feeling? What are your justifications for drinking? See if you notice a pattern. If a certain feeling often triggers an urge to drink, think about other ways you could deal with that emotion. Perhaps you could call a friend, meditate, or go for a walk instead.

GOOD

FOOD,

GOOD

Mood.

Thomas Carlyle

CURB YOUR
SWEET TOOTH

When you're feeling anxious, it's easy to think treating yourself with a chocolate bar or sugary snack will lift your spirits. Although it will give you a short burst of energy, your mood will soon crash, leaving you feeling low. To give your body the sweet taste it's craving, try eating naturally sweet foods such as carrots, berries, and coconut.

He who has health, has
hope; and he who has
hope, has everything.

Thomas Carlyle

WORRY
IS A

misuse

OF YOUR

imagination.

LES BROWN

Eat happy

We all know that eating protein is good for our bodies, especially after exercise. But did you know that

protein can make you feel happier too?

This is because foods like egg whites, fish, meat, soybeans, and cheese contain the amino acid tryptophan—a magic ingredient that your body turns into the hormone serotonin. This essential chemical

lifts your spirits, helps you sleep, and improves your memory,

so for a happier brain, try to include lots of protein-rich foods in your diet.

HYDRATE TO FEEL GREAT

If you're feeling worn out even though you've had plenty of sleep, the culprit could be dehydration. Drink plenty of liquids and eat foods with a high-water content, like oranges, watermelon, or yogurt. A quick indicator of your hydration is your pee. It should be a pale straw color—anything darker than this can be a sign that something's up, and it could be that you need to top up your water levels.

WORRIES GO DOWN BETTER WITH SOUP.

Jewish proverb

Look AFTER your TUMMY

It might seem odd, but having a healthy gut can actually affect the way you process your emotions. This is because the bacteria in your tummy help to turn certain foods into the happy hormone, serotonin—so the more good bacteria you have, the higher your serotonin level will be. Eat live yogurt and plenty of fruits, vegetables, and beans to keep your gut healthy and boost your mood.

Food is joy

Next time you have a meal, turn off the
TV and remove any other distractions
so you can really savor it. To enjoy
your food more, chew it carefully and
think about the tastes and textures of
what you are eating. You'll realize how
delicious it is.

ALL YOU NEED IS

love.

BUT A LITTLE

chocolate

NOW AND THEN DOESN'T HURT.

Charles M. Schulz

GET FIT,
GET
HAPPY

Stretches the back

Builds
upper body

Improves
concentration

Stimulates
the brain

START WITH A STRETCH

Instead of reaching for your phone, start the day with some simple yoga stretches. Set your alarm 10 minutes earlier than usual and find a space you can move in. First, kneel on all fours and round your back, with your head and bottom tucked in. Hold the pose for ten breaths. Then, straighten your back and legs to make an "A."

Energizes the
entire body

Opens
the chest

Strengthens
the legs

Develops
balance

shape, with your bottom in
the air—hold for another ten
breaths. Finally, move one foot
forward into a lunge. Slowly
lift your head and torso, and
stretch your arms to the ceiling,
palms facing towards each
other. This is "warrior pose."

An early morning walk is a blessing for the whole day.

Henry David Thoreau

GET YOUR HEART PUMPING

One of the best ways to beat worry is to get your heart pumping by doing high-energy exercises like running or aerobics. As well as being good for your body, it's a great way to relieve tension and stress, and it boosts your mood by flooding the brain with endorphins, which help fight stress.

Take in

Nature

What if there was a way to boost the stress-relieving benefits of exercise to make your workout even more beneficial? Luckily there is—exercising outdoors. Studies show that after spending even just 15 minutes in a natural setting we start to feel psychologically restored. Next time you go on a run, why not try jogging through a park or along the bank of a river instead of on the treadmill? As you run, think about your surroundings. What can you smell? How does the air feel on your face? Can you hear birds singing or trees rustling? What can you see?

When your body starts **moving,** your brain stops **whirring.**

TRUE ENJOYMENT COMES FROM ACTIVITY OF THE MIND AND EXERCISE OF THE BODY; THE TWO ARE EVER UNITED.

Wilhelm von Humboldt

Find a friend

It's always easier to keep up your enthusiasm when you're not on your own, so if you'd like to exercise more but struggle to gather the willpower, team up with a friend who can help you stay motivated. You could also look for local groups online—whether it's a running group, an exercise class, or a sports team. Many are cheap or free to join, and there are plenty of options for people of all abilities.

IF IT DOESN'T

CHALLENGE

YOU,

IT WON'T

CHANGE

YOU.

Fred DeVito

FOCUS ON
FEELING GOOD

When we exercise it's easy to focus on
becoming slimmer or more toned, but
this preoccupation with self-image can
have a negative impact on our mental
health. Instead, try to tune in to what
you're feeling. The next time you go for
a walk or run, instead of looking in the
mirror to see if your stomach is flatter,
take a few moments afterwards to think
about how the exercise made you feel.
Is your mind clearer? Are you happier,
or less stressed? Do you feel proud
of yourself for getting fit? Use these
observations and the promise of feeling
good to spur you on next time you don't
feel like exercising.

TAKE A

Challenge

If you're the type of person who needs a deadline to stay motivated, why not sign up for a challenge like a short run or swimming race to help keep you on track? The sense of achievement you get from finishing a race will do wonders for your mind.

The voice inside your head that says you can't do this is a liar.

Build your day around you

Our busy lives often get in the way of keeping fit.
So instead of joining a gym why not build exercise
into your day by getting off the bus a stop earlier,
or cycling to college or work? Studies show that
even short bursts of activity—such as a 10-minute
walk—can improve your fitness levels and will
leave you feeling great.

MOTIVATION

HELPS YOU START;
HABIT
KEEPS YOU GOING.

Jim Rohn

SLEEP
WELL,
FEEL
WELL

Sleep is the
best meditation.

Dalai Lama

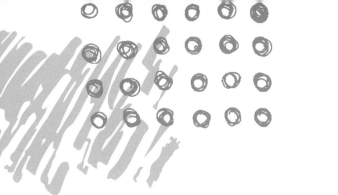

Hit the reset button

Sleep is an amazing thing. It can help lower blood pressure, decrease anxiety, and alleviate stress. But more often than not, it's something we take for granted or lose out on because other things in life get in the way. Try to make a good night's sleep one of your top priorities as it will lay a good foundation for you to feel happy and relaxed in the day ahead.

FIND YOUR MAGIC NUMBER

While 8 hours is the average amount of sleep an adult needs, it's important to remember that everyone is different. To find out how much you need, find a few days where you don't need to set an alarm. Go to bed at the same time each night, allow yourself to sleep for as long as you need and make a note of when you wake up. You may find you only need 7½ hours of sleep, or you may need 8½ or more. The perfect amount of sleep is however much you need to feel alert and happy during the day.

Create a sleep sanctuary

Our beds can sometimes become an extension of our other living areas —a place where we work, read, stream TV programs, chat on the phone, and even eat. But by doing all these things from the comfort of beneath our duvet, we begin to associate our beds with activity rather than sleep. This can make it difficult to drop off when we do eventually want to get some shut-eye. Instead, make your bedroom a restful sanctuary where sleep is the primary activity. Think about how to make your room a more peaceful space. Perhaps you could have soft lighting from a lamp or fairy lights, a soothing scent from a diffuser, or soft and breathable bedclothes.

Slow down,

UNWIND,

AND ALLOW YOURSELF
TO SLEEP.

Before four

It's no secret that tea and coffee can keep us awake, but you might not realize how long the effects take to wear off. Caffeine can stay in your system for 4 to 6 hours after being consumed, so if lights-out for you is around 10 or 11 o'clock in the evening, switch to herbal tea or water after 4 for a better night's sleep.

A good laugh and a long sleep are the two best cures.

Irish Proverb

HIT THE EXERCISE SWEET SPOT

Although the gym is a great stress buster, late-night sessions can keep you awake as your body will still be flooded with adrenaline when your head hits the pillow. For the best night's sleep, exercise between 4 o'clock and 7 o'clock in the evening.

HAVE A BEDTIME RITUAL

As much as we wish we could turn off our brains instantly, it takes time to wind down. If possible, put between 30 minutes and an hour aside for your bedtime ritual each night. Start by getting into your pajamas, washing your face, and cleaning your teeth. Doing this at the beginning means you won't wake yourself up by going to the bathroom later on. Dim the lights if you're able to, then spend the remaining time letting your brain wind down by listening to a podcast or an audiobook, writing in a journal, massaging in some body butter, or anything else that helps you relax, as long as it's without looking at a screen.

Tired minds
don't plan well.
SLEEP.
FIRST,
plan later.

Walter Reisch

WEEKEND WAKE-UPS

There's no better feeling than waking up after a good night's sleep and feeling refreshed. But, contrary to what we might think, lie-ins don't make up for lost sleep. In fact, they can actually disrupt your body clock and can end up making you feel worse rather than better. Instead, have a set wake-up time and stick to it every day of the week.

SLEEP MINDFULLY

If you struggle to fall asleep, try using mindfulness techniques. Lie in a comfortable position and close your eyes. Take a deep breath through your nose for five counts, then breathe out through your mouth for seven counts. Put one hand on your stomach and feel it rise and fall with each breath. Focus on how the bedclothes feel. Are they soft? Do you feel warm? Which parts of your body support your weight on the mattress? If any thoughts come into your head while you do this exercise, try to watch them float past like balloons rather than holding on to them. Soon you will drift off to the land of nod.

DIGITAL DETOX

The blue light from phones and tablets is very similar to natural morning light. When you see it, it switches your brain into "wake-up mode," which means that looking at screens before bed won't do you any favors. If you can, ban phones and tablets from the bedroom, or keep them on the other side of the room switched to silent mode to allow you and your mind some peace and quiet.

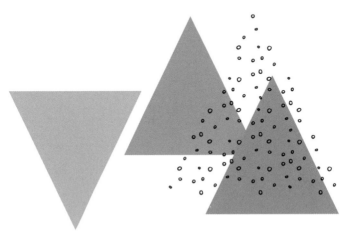

THERE IS A TIME FOR MANY WORDS, AND THERE IS ALSO A TIME FOR SLEEP.

Homer

HAVE A BEDTIME SNACK

There's nothing worse than hunger pangs when you're trying to sleep. To keep them at bay, try having a small snack an hour before bed. Choose a food that will release energy slowly, such as oatcakes, or have a glass of warm milk. Avoid chocolate as the caffeine and sugar will keep you awake.

SLEEP IS THE GOLDEN CHAIN THAT

TIES HEALTH AND OUR BODIES TOGETHER.

BE
POSITIVE

If you don't
like something,

change it.

If you can't change it,
change your

Maya Angelou

FIND YOUR TRIGGERS

One of the best ways to deal with anxiety is to find out what triggers it. Next time you feel anxious, stop and take a mental note of where you are, what you're doing, and who you're with. Do this every day until you start to notice a pattern. Perhaps you feel anxious around a certain family member, or perhaps a particular place or activity is the culprit.

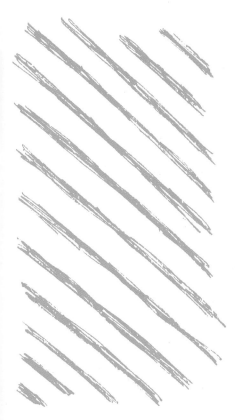

Once you've identified your trigger, think of five things you could do in the moment to reduce your stress.

Think about whether you need to make a long-term change, like looking for a new job or seeing a particular person less.

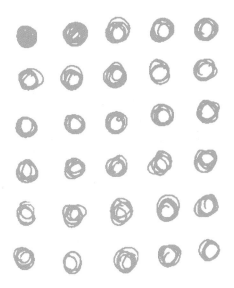

Wake up, smile, and tell yourself:

Today is my day.

Don't COMPARE

Social media makes
it easier than ever to
compare our lives to others', but
remember that most people only
show the highlight reel and that
everybody, no matter who they are,
has ups and downs. If you're feeling
low, focus on the good things in
your life, your own strengths,
and the achievements
you've made.

Accept what you can't control

There are two types of problem: ones we can solve and ones we can't. Do everything you can to tackle the problems you can solve and accept that the rest is out of your control. Knowing when to let go is a big step towards reducing tension in your life.

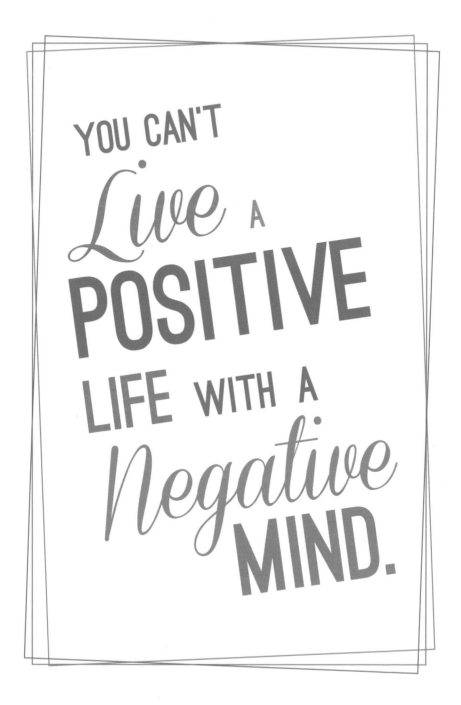

YOU CAN'T *Live* A POSITIVE LIFE WITH A *Negative* MIND.

Folks are usually about as
happy as they make up
their minds to be.

Anonymous

PRACTICE GRATITUDE

Have you ever noticed that some people seem happy no matter what life throws at them, and others find something to complain about regardless of how brilliant their life is? That's because our mindset is just as important as circumstance when it comes to feeling happy. The good news is there are easy ways to train your brain into thinking more positively. Next time you find yourself getting into a spiral of worry, list three things you're grateful for. You might want to keep a gratitude journal and write down a few things which made you happy at the end of each day.

BE PERFECTLY IMPERFECT

There's nothing wrong with aiming high, but seeking perfection in every aspect of your life will leave you feeling exhausted and unhappy. Even the cleverest and most successful people in the world aren't perfect human beings. Instead, allow yourself to make mistakes and don't beat yourself up about them—with a more relaxed approach to life will come a more relaxed mindset.

Try not to catastrophize

When you're worried, it's easy to get caught up thinking about the worst possible scenario. In fact it's something your brain automatically does to help keep you safe. But, while it can be helpful to be prepared, obsessing about it will make matters worse. Next time you find yourself worrying about a particular situation, ask yourself what is the absolute worst thing which could happen. Then list five things on a piece of paper which you could do to make it better. Then get on with your day and don't allow yourself to think about it again.

When I let go of what I am, I become what I might be.

Lao Tzu

Silence your inner critic

We all have an inner critic—that horrible voice in your head that puts you down and makes you doubt yourself. Next time you notice the voice, make note of what it says and ask yourself if you would speak that way to your best friend. It's likely that you wouldn't—so don't say it to yourself! Being kind in your thoughts and respecting yourself goes a long way to feeling calmer, more relaxed, and in control.

BE
HAPPY
WITH WHAT YOU HAVE AND ARE,
BE
Generous
WITH BOTH,
AND YOU DON'T HAVE TO HUNT FOR HAPPINESS.

William Gladstone

FOCUS ON THE

Present

Worrying about the future or about past events can stop us enjoying our lives in the present. Next time you're consulting your inner crystal ball, take a step back. Instead, think about what you can see, hear, smell, feel, and taste in the present moment.

THE REAL

gift

OF GRATITUDE IS THAT THE MORE *grateful* YOU ARE, THE MORE GRATEFUL YOU *become.*

LES BROWN

SLOW

DOWN

I JUDGE NO ONE
WHOM I'VE MET
ALONG THE WAY
BECAUSE IN A
SENSE WE WERE
ALL WOUNDED IN
OUR OWN WAYS.

Forrest Curran

IF YOU MISS THE
PRESENT MOMENT,
YOU MISS YOUR
APPOINTMENT
WITH LIFE.

Thích Nhất Hạnh

Visualize

One of the most effective ways to clear anxieties from your mind is to use the power of visualization. Take a few moments when you wake up to imagine everything in your day going perfectly. Picture getting everything you need to do finished on time and only having positive interactions with people. If any doubts or negative thoughts creep into your vision, push them to one side. You'll probably find your day goes much more smoothly and you will feel better equipped to handle anything that doesn't go to plan. Do this every morning and see what a difference it makes.

FORGET MULTITASKING

We often find ourselves doing a million things at once, and this can quickly become overwhelming. No matter how long your to-do list is, the best way to keep your stress at bay is to focus on one task at a time before moving on to the next one. You'll get things done more quickly and feel much more in control.

Savor

THE

MOMENT

LIVE SLOWLY

One way of feeling more zen is to take everyday tasks
a little more slowly. As you tidy up, enjoy the gradual
feeling of order and organization. Eat your dinner taking
time to savor each mouthful or take a shower and relish
the hot water and foamy bubbles of shampoo. Even just
taking a few moments extra to do these things can be
relaxing, and you'll learn to appreciate the small joys of
life and feel more positive.

MAKE CONNECTIONS

It's easy to focus on the material things in life to make you feel good, like buying new clothes or things for your home—and it's only natural to want these things since we're constantly being advertised to. But the happiest people in life focus on making their relationships with other people flourish. Instead of going shopping, invest time in the people you love, whether it's by taking the time to visit your family, or calling a friend who you haven't spoken to in a while, as it's human connections that will truly enrich your life and well-being.

Wherever
you
are,
be all
there.

Jim Elliot

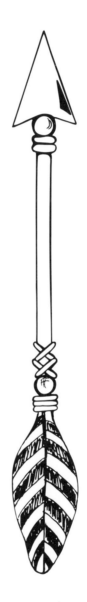

BE CHILDLIKE

In our busy lives it's easy to forget the carefree
attitude we had when we were children—but
it's never too late to start living that way again!
Whatever you're doing, remember to laugh and play
and don't be afraid not to take life too seriously.

Less do.

More

be.

LEARN TO
SAY NO

It's easy to wear yourself out by saying *yes* to people, whether it's an invite for a night out, an extra task for your boss, or a favor for a friend. But before saying *yes*, ask yourself: do I really have time to do this? Have I got the energy for it? If the answer is *no* to either of those questions, then don't be afraid to say so. Saying *no* to begin with is better than disappointing someone later when you have to cancel plans, or making a rushed attempt at a task. When your schedule is clearer you'll feel less stressed and have more energy for the things you do decide to do.

LIBERATION IS BEING WHOLLY AND
QUIETLY ALIVE, AWARE AND ALERT,
READY FOR WHATEVER MAY COME.

Bruce Lee

157

THE

HAPPIEST

PEOPLE

DON'T HAVE THE BEST
OF EVERYTHING;

THEY JUST MAKE

THE BEST OF
EVERYTHING.

Anonymous

Be a voice, not an echo.

Albert Einstein

EMBRACE CHANGE

The only thing in life which is constant is change. Try to remember that bad times don't last forever and whatever negative emotions you may be experiencing will also pass. Embracing the ebb and flow of life will help you to manage your feelings and help you approach any worries with a calmer frame of mind.

NATURAL THERAPIES

Soak away your troubles

There's nothing like sinking into a hot bath at the end of the day to bring you a feeling of calm. Adding Epsom salts can make your soak even more beneficial as they top up your levels of magnesium, which is known to decrease anxiety.

AROMATHERAPY

Aromatherapy takes advantage of the effect certain scents have on our limbic system, triggering different emotions. Lavender is said to help you sleep and reduce anxiety, while jasmine, ylang-ylang, and bergamot are also calming scents. Try burning a candle with one of these essential oils in, or taking a bath using an aromatic bath oil. However, be aware that if you are using essential oils for the first time it is advisable to consult your doctor first.

Time spent on yourself is the
best kind of investment.

Shiatsu

Shiatsu has been around for thousands of years, helping relieve tension and muscle stress in its fans. Stemming from the Japanese term for "finger pressure," shiatsu is a combination of massage and stretching which aims to reduce anxiety. Many therapists and health centers offer this service, so look online to find practitioners near you.

WHATEVER YOU'RE WORRIED ABOUT,

YOU'RE

BIGGER

THAN THE WORRIES.

Dalai Lama

Find whatever it is that makes

your heart
sing and
do it
every day.

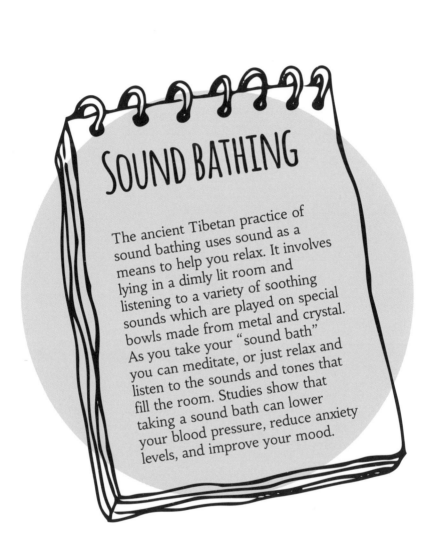

SOUND BATHING

The ancient Tibetan practice of sound bathing uses sound as a means to help you relax. It involves lying in a dimly lit room and listening to a variety of soothing sounds which are played on special bowls made from metal and crystal. As you take your "sound bath" you can meditate, or just relax and listen to the sounds and tones that fill the room. Studies show that taking a sound bath can lower your blood pressure, reduce anxiety levels, and improve your mood.

The time to

RELAX

IS WHEN YOU DON'T
HAVE TIME FOR IT.

Acupuncture

This traditional Chinese practice has been around for thousands of years. Although there are relatively few scientific studies on it, what we do know is that it releases happy hormones and natural painkillers into the bloodstream, which help to relieve anxiety. According to the *British Medical Journal*, it's also one of the safest medical treatments available.

Your inner landscape determines your outer life.

Heidi DuPree

Try massage

Have you ever noticed that when
you're stressed, your back and
shoulders begin to ache? This
is because when you're feeling
under pressure the muscles in your
shoulders and upper back become
tense. Having regular massages can
ease the tension in your back by
soothing the muscles. However,

even if your shoulders don't feel achy, having a massage has been shown to increase the levels of oxytocin and serotonin in the brain, making you feel happier and more relaxed. What's more, having a massage can help clear your mind by giving you at least half an hour of quiet contemplation.

Sauna

Stepping into a sauna is an excellent way to make you feel good both in body and mind. As well as being a warm, quiet space where you're able to press pause on the rest of the world, saunas relax your muscles and help your body to flush out toxins through sweating. They can also reduce levels of the stress hormone cortisol, making you feel more relaxed and reducing feelings of frustration.

STOP worrying and START living.

Herbal tea

There are few things more comforting than a steaming mug of tea. But replacing strong caffeinated tea with herbal tea can have even more benefits for your mind and body. As well as being soothing, caffeine-free, and having properties that could help to boost your immune system, teas containing chamomile, passion flower, valerian root, and peppermint all have calming properties.

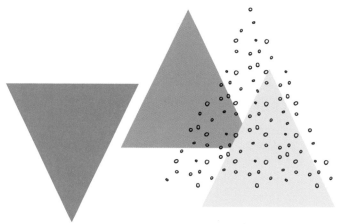

**WORRY
NEVER ROBS
TOMORROW
OF ITS
SORROW, IT
ONLY SAPS
TODAY OF
ITS JOY.**

Leo Buscaglia

SEEKING
HELP

Don't be afraid to ask for help

It's natural to feel worried sometimes, and often a good diet, exercise, plenty of sleep, and a positive attitude can help you get through. But if you're finding it difficult to cope with your anxiety, and it's causing you problems in your day-to-day life, there are many resources out there to help you. Read on to find out some of the steps available to you, or talk to your doctor.

THINGS HAPPEN TO YOU

BUT THEY DON'T HAVE TO HAPPEN TO YOUR SOUL.

Jennifer Lawrence

CHALLENGING
THOUGHTS

If you're still having difficulty with
unwanted thoughts and feelings,
it might be worth considering
cognitive behavioral therapy (CBT).
CBT is a therapy that helps you to
replace negative thought patterns,
which cause distress, with more
constructive ones. Over time, this
helps to improve your overall well-
being and allows you to develop
a more positive mindset. Consult
your doctor if you would like to
explore this option further.

EXPOSURE THERAPY

It's only natural to avoid doing things which cause anxiety, but gradual exposure to the things which scare you can help you realize the reality isn't as bad as you imagined. Exposure therapy is one of the most effective treatments for anxiety. If you would like to learn more about the different options for you, consult your doctor.

Do the things that

challenge you.

Hypnosis

When you think of hypnosis, you may have an image of someone in a trance, possibly doing something ridiculous such as dancing around like a chicken. However, the reality is very different. Most of us go into a state of hypnosis several times a day, like when you're walking a familiar route and suddenly realize you're home, or when you're on the bus and start daydreaming. In hypnotherapy, the therapist helps you relax into this state so that the conscious, critical part of your mind switches off. Then they speak to the unconscious part of your brain. For some people, this can help build self-esteem and quiet fears.

APPLIED RELAXATION

Sometimes when you're in a stressful situation it's hard to know how to make the waves of anxiety pass. Applied relaxation is a technique some therapists teach to help you get through moments of panic. It involves learning to relax the muscles in the body individually to help you feel calmer. You may need to practice this a few times to get the hang of it. Once you've learned how to do this, you can use the technique to help you stay calm the next time a stressful situation arises, and maintain that feeling throughout the day.

Don't worry.
Be happy.

OUR *Wounds* ARE OFTEN *the* OPENINGS

INTO THE BEST AND MOST *Beautiful* PART OF US.

David Richo

If you're interested in finding out more
about our books, find us at:

WWW.SKYHORSEPUBLISHING.COM

IMAGE CREDITS